A DEVELOPER'S GUIDE TO JOB OFFERS

by John M. P. Knox

Table of Contents

CHAPTER ONE

Introduction

You're here because you're contemplating a new job. Maybe you already have an offer in your hand, or maybe you're just trying to do the research before you interview. Either way, I think this book will help you look at the golden promise of a new job with more rational eyes.

This book has been edited from a series of essays I originally published on EngineeringAdventure.com. My friends seemed to like them and find them useful in choosing a job and negotiating an offer. I've used these same techniques to manage my career. It's worked pretty well: I've worked my way up the ranks by carefully picking each new job. Even though I've made mistakes and had large setbacks, I now make more than double the salary I had as a lowly new college grad.

I've switched jobs 6 times since I've left college. Each time has been a trade-off: some good and some bad came of it. Even the worst jobs opened up new doors and career paths that led to even greater success. The worst jobs can also teach you a lot about how to be a better person — something which might be more important to your career than technical developer skills.

In the following pages, you'll see that the majority of my focus is on the financial aspects of the job offer. Don't let that confuse you. Money is important and money mistakes can cause a lot of problems, but happiness is the key to happiness. Don't let a few thousand dollars a year trick you into working for a crappy boss or giving up hobbies that make you happy. Don't pick a job that you don't believe in either. It's not worth it for a little more money.

When you get an offer, look at the finances. Make sure they will cover your bills, will leave enough to build savings, and will leave you in a better place than you are now. Then make sure that the job will challenge you, will make Monday mornings interesting. Double check that you like the people you'll be working with and working for.

Also make sure that the work and culture aligns with your personal values. That doesn't mean that you should work with clones; healthy, vibrant teams carry a variety of view points. The greatest learning comes from considering outside beliefs and ideas. I mean that you should avoid a job that will ask you to do something you think is unethical or immoral.

Most of all, imagine a typical day at the new job and decide if it feels better than your alternatives.

To help you with the financial considerations, I've put together a Google Spreadsheet that you can use to weigh the important financial considerations of a job offer. Even though a job offer letter has only three blanks (i.e. Name, Salary, Equity Grant), you'll see that there are many more variables you'll need to consider.

You can see what it looks like below, populated with sample salary data:

Item	Current Income & Expense	NYC offer Income & Expenses	San Francisco Income & Expenses	Instructions
pretax income (monthly)	$8,333.33	$14,166.67	$14,166.67	use a tax calculato
after tax income (monthly)	$5,963.89	$8,276.67	$8,403.36	
Mortgage/rent (monthly)	$1,200.00	$5,000.00	$4,600.00	Use zillow or a sim
Home/Renter insurance (monthly)	$150.00	$63.00	$63.00	
Property Taxes (monthly)	$403.50	$0.00	$0.00	If you plan to own y
Estimated value of equity (monthly)	$0.00	$0.00	$0	Unless you're awar
Health Insurance Costs (monthly)	$0.00	$0.00	$0.00	If you will be contri
lunch expense (monthly)	$0.00	$0.00	$0.00	Ignore this unless c
other benefits (monthly)	$0.00	$0.00	$0.00	a common belefit b
401k matching (monthly)	$0.00	$0.00	$0.00	only include this if y
Annual Bonus (monthly)	$0.00	$0.00	$0.00	If you're sure to get
Annual Bonus less taxes (monthly)	$0.00	$0.00	$0.00	To get the bonus a
signon bonus after tax (monthly)	$0.00	$0.00	$0.00	Like the annual bor
monthly take home:	$4,226.14	$3,212.67	$3,540.26	The monthly take h
improvement over current compensation:	$0.00	-$1,013.48	-$305.88	This is the net char
private equity "valuation"	$96,000.00	$0.00	$0.00	I consider approxim
publicly traded stock	$0.00	$40,000	$0	Publicly traded sto
vacation days	Unlimited	10	15	I put this here to re

This table helps you compare compensation on a montly basis. In my example, I'm comparing a $100,000 salary in Austin to a $170,000 salary in San Francisco and

If you'd like to get access to the

spreadsheet, you can visit http://eepurl.com/9c5z5 and fill out the form. I'll send you an email with the link. You'll get an occasional email about building an awesome career in software development, If you'd rather not, you can immediately unsubscribe after you get the spreadsheet. My feelings won't be hurt. Much.

I'd love to hear what you think about this book, and what other topics you think I should write about. You can reach me on twitter as @WindAddict. On EngineeringAdventure.com, you can find my essays on topics like careers, recruiting, software, business, marketing, and even photography.

Best Wishes,

John M. P. Knox
Austin, TX
January 19, 2015

CHAPTER TWO

Understanding Risk

If you're considering taking a new job, you first have to figure out the risk involved in the move. Anytime you switch jobs, you're in the position of leaving a well-understood, stable situation for a poorly understood new position. You have to learn about and deal with a new boss, a new role, new coworkers, and a new environment... and compared to your old job, you understand very little about these things. If the new job doesn't work out, it's doubtful that you can simply return to your previous job. Understanding the ways things can go wrong can help you correctly decide how you should be compensated for them.

Switching jobs is like moving into a new home. The new house seems great until you move in and discover that there is a roach infestation, the water pressure only allows one shower at a time, and the neighbors have a garage band that practices until 2 AM every Monday morning. It won't take too many nasty surprises to make you feel home-sick for your last place.

Luckily, unlike a job search, when buying a new home there are standard steps people use to help reduce their risk. It's rare to buy a home without an appraisal and a home inspection. Even those steps miss things, like the 120 volt death trap I discovered in my house's attic. Just because a home is new and has passed inspection doesn't mean there aren't a pair of exposed live wires where a light switch should be.

Just like with a house inspection, even the most heavily researched new job can hold many unpleasant surprises. And unfortunately, most people don't do enough research.

Maybe your new manager will make you a scapegoat for a failure that has been simmering for two years. Maybe your new teammates won't pull their weight. Maybe you're given an impossible deadline. Maybe everyone will get mandatory pay cuts just a few months after you arrive. There's just no way of predicting everything that can affect you in your new job.

For instance, when I worked at AMD, every salaried employee received a mandatory 10% (or more) pay-cut[1]. At the time (and still today), AMD was a Fortune 500 company. Even though it's a large, publicly-traded company, it is still unpredictable. And if a large company is unpredictable, just imagine what can happen at a smaller company.

Don't forget that a new employer

can simply fire you if you don't work out. Some companies even have an explicit probationary period in which you can legally be dismissed for any reason–or for no reason–without severance pay. If you're terminated, you'll have to be pre-pared to make ends meet while you look for a new job. Except for a few weeks of salary, the employer will be no worse off than they were before hiring you. If you end up hating your new employer, you'll have to endure it for as long as it takes to search for another job.

I've only reviewed a few aspects of risk here, but there are many more risks inherent in taking a new job. (Keep your eyes out for future posts on specific types of risk and how to assess them.) You probably will never have a full un-derstanding of the risk at a job before you've worked there for some time. Usu-ally you can't just switch back to your old

life. It only makes sense to get compensated for that risk up front.

---

[1] http://www.cnet.com/news/amd-
to-trim-1100-jobs-initiate-temporary-
pay-cuts/

CHAPTER THREE

The Cost of Living

If you're moving for your job, I suggest a two-pronged approach to researching the change in expense. The first and quickest method is to use a cost of living calculator to see what the value of your current salary (plus 10%!) is in your new city. In order to feel the most confident about the results, I use a variety of them.

The second part of your research is to investigate the actual expenses you will have in the new city. Since housing costs are typically one of the biggest expenses, I use tools like Zillow and Craigslist to get an idea of what housing costs, and what the more common forms of available housing are.

By investigating the expenses using two different methods, you can be more confident with what you discover, and also learn a bit more about the city you're considering moving to. Maybe your prospective employer is based in a more expensive neighborhood than the cost of living calculators anticipate. Like-wise, your idea of middle-class housing may differ quite a bit from the norm in the city you're contemplating.

In San Francisco, for instance, the most available kinds of housing are apartments and condos. I suggest look-ing at houses that are both similar in size to your current home and near where you would work. You should also consider if you actually would want to live in the area near work! If the nearest area you're comfortable is a long commute away from the office, you should take that into consideration.

Transportation costs like a long com-mute, daily tolls, or expensive parking can also rack up.. Based on your housing research and personal preferences, you should already have some ideas about how you would get to work: walking, driving, busses, subways, ferries, etc. It is worth investigating the costs of transportation, gas, parking, tolls, subway passes, and other transportation expenses associated with your prospective new job.

A common negotiating gambit that recruiters use is to suggest that you take a lower salary and live in a less expensive suburb, or "bedroom community." The term refers to towns where the primary activity is sleeping and breadwinners work elsewhere. If you don't mind a commute, and you aren't looking for a neighborhood with an active culture, this might be fine. However, don't fall into the trap of letting the recruiter tell you where to live. Just because it's a short commute to New Jersey from New York

City doesn't mean you should have to take a New Jersey salary for a New York job.

If you're getting pressured to accept a salary based on living in another city, I suggest firmly but politely telling the recruiter that you've researched those options, but they don't meet your needs. You shouldn't feel guilty saying no to being told where to live or how much compensation you should accept. Feeling brave? Take a chance and ask where the CEO lives. They usually don't have a long commute (unless they live in a nicer place than the business).

Another category of other direct expenses to research are taxes. Federal income tax, state income tax, city income tax (hello NYC), property tax, and sales taxes... the list seemingly goes on and on, and different states have different rules.

Keep in mind that even if you feel like you have a handle on federal income tax, with a new job you might move up or down to a different tax bracket.

The best way I've found to research taxes in the US is with Paycheck City[1]. Paycheck City is a free tool I've used when I was consulting to help calculate salary taxes for myself.

To use Paycheck City, you need to select a state. From there, there are two different ways to consider the tax situation. The first method is to examine the annual perspective, which is how people commonly discuss offers. Enter your annual salary in the Gross Pay field, set Gross Pay Type to Annually, and then fill out the form. Note that if the state has cities with personal income tax, you'll be asked for your work address to see if you qualify. You'll get an amount as if you were paid once a year.

The other way to use Paycheck City to consider your economic situation is to look at it from a monthly perspective. I think this is also useful because rents, credit card bills, utilities, are all monthly expenses. You'll have an easier time thinking of the realities on a monthly basis. To see a monthly perspective, enter your monthly salary into the Gross Pay field, and then select "Per Pay Period" for Gross Pay Type, and select a "Pay Frequency" of monthly. Fill out the rest of the form as before.

When you hit the Calculate button, you'll see approximately how much money you'll get in your paycheck after taxes. You can take that number and compare it to your last paycheck at your current job — correcting for cost of living differences, naturally.

---

[1] http://www.paycheckcity.com/calculator/salary/

CHAPTER FOUR

Comparing Salaries

Salary: you might not think it requires much thought-- and if your offer just takes you down the street, you may be right. However, you'll need to move cross-country, or even to a different city, you have some comparison work to do. Location significantly impacts the value of a dollar.

To start with, the value of your new salary should probably be at least 10% more than the value of your current salary. By way of comparison, the typical raise when moving companies is 10-20%[1]. If you didn't disclose your current salary during salary negotiations, you may do better than that. (I know I have!)

But what is the value of the salary? It's not simply the dollar amount. Even though people say "the world is flat", the value of money is quite geographic. A salary, and the value of that salary really depends on where you live.

The cost of living varies greatly from city to city. For instance, I live in Austin Texas. I own a moderately sized house in the city with a backyard, a kitchen, three bedrooms, 2.5 bathrooms, etc etc. I pay about $1000 a month in mortgage and property tax expenses. If I lived in San Francisco with my current salary, I wouldn't be able to afford a home at all. Renting a decent two bedroom apartment would cost around $4500 a month! I've heard you sometimes have to interview just to get an apartment there!

If an employer wanted me to move to San Francisco, would they have to pay me the previously mentioned 10-20% more? (That would be (4500 - 1000) * 12 = $42,000 more per year.) Absolutely not. They would have to pay even more:

income taxes would eat up much of that, not to mention staples like food, gasoline, utilities, and more. (More on taxes later.)

For my purposes, when I discuss the value of a salary, I mean the equivalent amount of money in your current city. A lot of the time, converting a salary in a new city to the equivalent value in your home city will make the comparison more familiar to you.

Salary Statistics

Never consider average geographic salaries for your position unless the average is well above the value you currently make. The same thing goes for average national salaries. So what if the average mobile software developer in New York City makes $169,000? If the value of your current salary in NYC dollars is $328,000, an average salary won't make you smile.

Another issue with average salaries is that you know very little about the statistical distribution of salaries[2]. For all you know, the salaries distribute bimodally: a group that makes $100,000 or lower (i.e. the suckers), and a group that makes $200,000 or more (i.e. the winners). Perhaps most developers make above the average, and a few low-paid outliers hold the numbers down[3]. Knowing the average helps, but it doesn't prove that a salary far from the average is ridiculous.

Average salaries are also lagging indicators. For instance, if there suddenly is a lot of demand for developers, salaries might go through the roof. Even so, the average salary data will reflect the obsolete situation until the next survey. The salary (and cost of living) data can be out of date quickly.

Finally, average salaries rely on accurate job titles. Job titles for software positions aren't very well defined. Some companies have one title: Software Developer. Some have nine: software developer 1, software developer 2, software developer 3, senior software developer 1, senior software developer 2, senior software developer 3, Member of Technical Staff, Senior Member of Technical Staff, Fellow. Multiple levels of experience tend to get glommed together in the statistics. Developers fresh from college might get lumped in with developers with thirty eight years of experience.

Also consider that developers with different experience and specialities may rate higher or lower salaries. Open GL developers might make more than Perl developers. Or maybe the other way around. Either way, if everyone is a "software developer" it isn't any help to you.

The lack of readily available data on this is probably why consulting firms make lots of money helping companies sort out this impossible mess of how much they should pay their employees.

Don't let average salaries mess with your head. A bad offer is a bad offer, even if the average salary data makes it look good by comparison. An average salary is just one number trying to hide a complex reality.

Consultant or Contractor Rates

In the United States, asking folks about their salary is considered taboo. I don't know how this came about, but it can make it difficult to do field research on salaries. Fortunately, the issue of contracting rates seems to be a little less taboo. I frequently ask my consultant peers what they think the typical prevailing rates are. None of them seem very upset by the question.

Consulting rates are usually hourly, by the day, or by the week. Multiply that number by the appropriate units to calculated the revenue for a fully-loaded year of consulting. From there, I usually divide that number by two and consider that the equivalent employee salary. This is a very rough approximation, but it can be a useful way to consider your value.

Why do I divide the annualized consulting rate and divide it by two? Because that's something a friend told me once. It's a gross simplification of the realities of business: the costs of health insurance, employee vacation, other benefits, the cost of acquiring customers, the lack of revenue between clients, and other expenses. Based on my consulting experience, I think you can have costs closer to 1/3 of revenue, but the revenue isn't necessarily steady.

As an aside, consultants and contractors in your field are a great career resource since they tend to have experience with multiple companies, and they have a more direct understanding of what companies really value.

---

[1] http://www.forbes.com/sites/cameronkeng/2014/06/22/employees-that-stay-in-companies-longer-than-2-years-get-paid-50-less/

[2] http://en.wikipedia.org/wiki/Anscombe's_quartet

[3] http://en.wikipedia.org/wiki/One-dollar_salary

CHAPTER FIVE

Benefits

A new job is about more than salary and title: there are a variety of expected benefits, like retirement, insurance, and vacation, that can dramatically affect your assessment of an offer.

Retirement Accounts

One often-overlooked benefit is the 401k or SEP IRA, especially if the employer contributes towards those retirement funds. Don't let recruiters give you a sob story about being too small for the 401k either. The SEP IRA is like a 401k for small businesses. Even my 1-person company had one when I was consulting. These are useful tools to help you save for retirement and defer paying income taxes.

I don't consider the 401k part of compensation unless the employer offers matching contributions. A typical matching contribution might be 50% of the first 4%. If the matching contributions have a vesting period of more than a few months, I consider it a gimmick to keep you from leaving, and I don't consider it part of compensation.

Employee Stock Purchase Plan

An employee stock purchase plan (ESPP) is a way for employees to deduct a fixed amount from their paycheck each month and invest it in their company stock. Typically the employee gets a significant discount on the market price of the stock. One of my former employers offered a 20% discount on the closing price of their stock on the first or last day of the quarter (whichever was lower).

In my experience, only a limited percentage of your salary can be invested in the ESPP.

Vacation

Vacation. Two weeks of vacation (i.e. 10 days) is the bare minimum amount most companies offer software developers. I think it's a miserly amount. I would try negotiating for 20 days of paid vacation, since 10 days is less than 3% of a year. Who wants to spend 97% of their life working 40+ hours a week?

The baseline value for a vacation day is the salary divided by 260 (52 weeks * 5 days). I value vacation days at least twice as much as their salary value. You can make more money, but you can't make more time.

Some companies offer "unlimited" vacation. The word unlimited means "no limits" to humans, but "zero" to many employers. Even in companies with good intentions, unlimited vacation policies can create peer pressure to take less vacation, as this essay written from the perspective of a founder describes[1]. If you want to read even more on the subject, this essay thoroughly evaluates the pros and cons of unlimited policies[2].

If your employer uses the word unlimited, make sure to get it in writing. Keep in mind that you might have to really stand up for yourself to take a reasonable amount of vacation. I would ask the manager and recruiter how many days of vacation the typical developer takes per year. If the number seems good, save it somewhere safe for later negotiations when you want a two-week vacation.

Holidays

US companies typically offer 10 or 11

holidays per year. Unless your offer doesn't meet this expectation, it's proba- bly not a point of comparison. I think some employers offer "floating holidays", which are nice since you're not forced to travel or go to the beach when it's crowded. If they offer 0 holidays, then they're being sneaky and expect you to use your vacation days.

Sick Days

Some jobs dictate how many days you're allowed to be sick. Others will let you take as many sick days as you need provided that it doesn't meet the defini- tion of short term disability. Typically they offer insurance for that case. Other com- panies lump their sick days in with vaca- tion, which seems like a bad idea since it encourages the sick to infect their coworkers. Except in the unlimited case, you'll need to make some estimates and see if you're going to lose vacation days (or pay) when you're sick.

Insurance

Medical insurance, dental insurance, life insurance, accidental death and dis-memberment, short term disability, and long term disability are all common ben-efits offered by companies of all sizes. Some companies will cover the monthly cost of all these types of insurances. Others will require employees to con-tribute some fraction of the cost out of their paycheck. In some cases, depend-ing on your age and health, it's cheaper to get your own coverage.

Recruiters may make it sound like the question of health insurance can be an-swered with a "yes" or "no," but that's an oversimplification. Every company that offers insurance should have a few sheets of paper documenting their costs and coverage. Ask for it, especially if you need coverage for more than yourself. Because each company has to negotiate their own health insurance, the plans are almost unique.

---

[1] http://www.paperplanes.de/2014/12/10/from-open-to-minimum-vacation-policy.html

[2] http://jacobian.org/writing/unlimited-vacation/

CHAPTER SIX

Extra Perks

Besides the benefits you expect, many businesses offer perks above and beyond mere vacation time. By factoring in these benefits, you can get a clearer idea of how much aspects of your new job will cost and whether or not these benefits actually benefit you.

Lunch and Snacks

When I worked at AMD a long time ago, my department decided to make our vending machines free. Like the other buildings, we had a coke machine and one of those snack machines with the spirals that sometime would leave your bag of Hot Fries dangling instead of pushing it into the tray. Unlike the other buildings, money wasn't required to dispense anything. We all thought it was an amazing benefit, and I put on six pounds eating too many bags of Cheetos.

It was so cool that folks in other departments would risk getting chewed out by our director to get free diet cokes.

When I later moved to Freescale, I was shocked to discover that they didn't even offer free coffee. A few enterprising engineers banded together to form coffee co-ops, but the non-members had to either scrounge up their own materials or visit the on-site Seattle's Best Coffee.

Today, it's becoming more common for software firms to offer free catered lunches, fresh fruit, and gourmet snacks to their employees. I think this is a pretty good benefit for both employees and the employer, but the value to you may depend on your lunch habits. If you like to bring your own lunch and eat at your desk, it might have no value to you. If you enjoy eating with your coworkers, and don't want to pack your own lunch, it could save you lots of time and maybe a couple thousand dollars a year.

The calculation is pretty easy, just take into account your vacation and holidays and any cost of living differences. For example:

46 weeks * 5 days * $10 per lunch = $2,300

Transportation and Parking

It is fairly common for businesses in the San Francisco area to have private busses that drive you to and from your home. They often feature free coffee and wifi. But don't assume that they are a cure for a long commute! I've heard that some companies only run the busses twice a day: once to work and once from work. Some companies arrange the schedule so that riders have to put in nearly twelve hour days. Be sure to ask questions so that you don't become a bus slave.

Some companies also will pay for passes to use public transportation. If taking public transportation makes sense for you, that could be a nice benefit.

Another benefit (which might reflect a cost of living expense too), is parking. If an employer is in an urban area a free parking lot isn't a given. Some employers have contracts with parking garages to offer their employees free or low-cost parking. If you're planning to drive to work, parking can be a significant expense. If you're planning to live near work, free parking might make owning a car more practical.

These benefits are nice, but probably

don't provide a huge value unless they help you go carless.

Relocation

If you're moving from one city to another to take a job, you may be offered relocation. This is generally offered as a choice of lump sum, or a package covered by the employer. The package usually means that the company hires movers for you, although sometimes they will also pay for other expenses: travel costs to visit the area before moving, closing costs to sell your house, corporate housing for a few weeks in the new city.

Relocation is really about breaking even on the move, so it is more of a concern when it doesn't exist, or if it is inadequate to your needs.

CHAPTER SEVEN

Equity

Though it may seem daunting, equity is actually really simple. All you have to do is make sure you get as much as you already have at your current company, or more (in supposed dollar value, based on the last investment). Unless the company has filed for IPO or is publicly traded, value the equity at zero. Don't accept equity for a salary of lower value.

Lots of people will disagree with the value of zero. I plan to write more about this because it is a complex topic. Most equity in private companies is so encumbered that it has little or no real value. In any case, there typically isn't enough liquidity to accurately value it.

Unless the company is publicly traded, I see stock, stock options, and restricted stock units (RSUs) as an incentive, not compensation. An incentive is something that helps align your interests with the interests of the company. Debatably, it can also serve as a motivational tool.

Even if the stock is public, that doesn't mean that it will keep its value over the next couple of years while it vests. When I last worked at AMD, the stock price was around $7.50 per share. Now in October of 2014 it's about $3.00. The S&P 500 has increased in value almost as much as AMD has lost value over that same time period. Holding a large amount of your compensation in one undiversified equity is a very risky thing.

Compensation is an exchange of value. You trade one thing of value for another thing of value. Equity is different.

The Investment Metaphor for Equity

Imagine that one day you get an unexpected phone call from someone named Pat. You've never talked to Pat before, but Pat has an amazing opportunity for you. If you jump in now, you'll get in before everyone else! Pat wants you to buy stock in a company working on the future of envelope technology. TongueCut Inc. and their safety envelopes are going to be huge! Not only is it impossible to get a lip or tongue injury with their new envelope technology, Pat explains, but they're working on flavored adhesives and have 14 envelope patents pending. If you want in — and of course you want in — you only have to invest $40,000. So what do you say?

I think most software developers I know would say "no thanks!" But at least some of them would gladly take a $40,000 paycut in exchange for restricted stock units in an unproven startup.

The investment in the envelope company might actually be a better deal since presumably Pat isn't selling restricted shares!

The Fishing Co-op Metaphor for Equity

Imagine that instead of developing software, you fish for a living. Instead of selling your fish on the market, you join a fishing co-op. The co-op has an interesting deal. You and the other co-op members deliver all your catch to the warehouse every day. The leaders of the co-op then trade or sell all the fish on behalf of the co-op.

Some days the leaders decide that they should spend the co-op money to buy new fishing gear, pay rent on the warehouse, that the division of shares should be changed, or that they should give some fish away. At the end of the month, the remaining funds of the co-op are split among the members according to the number of shares each has. It might be zero. If the co-op can figure out a way to make the fish more valuable, or if you have a disproportionate number of shares, you might make more money than you would have as a lone fisherman.

Is that compensation? I don't think so. It's more of a form of collectivism with totalitarian rule. Also note that the only thing which you can control is how much effort you put into your fishing. The leaders can eat all of the fish, they can give shares of the co-op to lazy friends, they can take a loan against the co-op to buy a Super Bowl commercial.

Now this metaphor isn't perfect, but hopefully it illustrates just how little value the stock of a private company can have, unless you own enough to have control (e.g. a seat on the board of directors).

My Equity Experience

If you're trying to figure out how to evaluate an equity offer, maybe my experience can help. Years ago, I gave up more than half my salary for a chance to work at an interesting startup. Replacing that salary was options that gave me ownership in a few percent of that company. Less than a year into the project, I saw issues that I thought would hurt our chances for success. I tried to persuade the CEO to make some changes, like talking to more than one VC for funding and working more to develop interest in the product. He wasn't very interested in my opinion. After I quit, I heard that the company let the staff go when funds ran out. I still own the stock, which hasn't earned me a dime and probably can't be sold.

I think this perfectly illustrates how even holding actual shares of a private stock doesn't give you any control. I couldn't change the course of the company even though I could talk to the CEO every day, and I held more than 1% of the stock! And unlike a shareholder of a public company, I don't receive quarterly reports on the status of the business.

Even equity in more successful startups offers relatively few rewards. Although I have heard of founders being able to cash in some of their equity during funding rounds, it seems like a very rare option for employees.

As a minority shareholder, I have very few rights, and the shares are mostly useless. And that's why I believe that the value of equity in startups is a myth that usually benefits the biggest owners of a company, not the employees.

CHAPTER EIGHT

Details and Traps

There are a number of other factors you have to consider before accepting a new job.

Recruiter Gambits

Some recruiters try to sell their equity by claiming that in the past employees were allowed to sell some of their shares after funding rounds. I think that's a great way to let employees get value from their shares. However, there isn't any way to know if that will ever happen again, or if you will be allowed to partici-pate. Issues like vesting schedules, the class of stock you have, your seniority, and your contract can prevent you from selling when others might be allowed to.

Another key to understanding your equity is getting a copy of the equity agreement. I've made the mistake of accepting a job offer before doing this, and when I eventually saw them, the terms of the agreement were quite surprising to me. Among other things, the stock units had an expiration date. If they expire before the company is sold or makes a public offering, the equity returns to the company and my value is zero.

With those terms, it hardly feels like "my" equity at all.

The kind of equity you'll probably be offered is worth a lot less than the equity the founders and investors have, but recruiters will tell you that your shares are worth what the last investors paid. I find these claims outrageous. Not only is it unlikely that you would receive the same preferred class of shares that investors have, you also have far less control of the company.

Unless you're an accredited investor with cash to spare, you can't invest in a more diversified portfolio of private companies like most investors would. This puts you at a significant disadvantage to the investors, who may have invested because they are specifically looking to invest in risky growth companies that have a chance at 10x or 100x returns. And it seems like those venture funded companies fail about 75% of the time[1].

It's also important to know what preferred stock can mean. In some cases, the investors have negotiated a guaranteed return, called a liquidity preference. These preferences mean that the investor gets to take some multiple of their investment out of the value of any sale of the company. If the investor invested $1 million with a 3x liquidity preference, then they get to remove $3 million from any deal in addition to their split of the remainder based on the shares they hold.

I imagine liquidity preferences are an intentionally confusing tool to help investors, and not employees profit from a successful startup[2]. You can ask your recruiter or hiring manager about the financial structure of the company, but I wouldn't count on their knowledge of the situation. It's not like public company where investor disclosures are publicly available. I'm sure there are many other tricks investors use that I'm not aware of.

Some companies will have a more credible explanation for their shares value because they have filed for IPO or publicly announced a merger or acquisition. Even if the company has filed for IPO or some other liquidity event, keep in mind that it might change its plans. Just google for "cancels IPO!" There is also no way of knowing how the shares will be valued at the time you're able to sell them. You'll almost certainly not be allowed to sell your shares immediately when the IPO or transaction occurs[3].

To sum up, I almost always value the equity component of an offer at zero. Equity is a great incentive to align your interests with the company so that you'll share in it's success. Its contractual caveats, vesting schedule, and lack of liquidity or control make it a poor substitute for cash. Ultimately you buy food and pay rent with cash, not equity.

Bonus Plans

Bonus plans and profit-sharing plans are motivational devices that can be almost anything. Like equity, the value of a bonus plan involves lots of wishful thinking. It's a lottery that's held once or more a year.

When negotiating at one place, I was told that one employee purchased a new Porsche with last year's bonus. I never got a large enough bonus to buy a used Volkswagen, much less a sports car, at that place. I later heard that he had been saving for that car for years and the bonus just made it happen faster. Never take the recruiter's word on these things at face value.

The nice thing about bonus plans is that there is often documentation to go along with them. I got an offer letter at a different business that laid out the bonus plan rules. Much to my surprise, the bonus was capped to 15% of the base salary. Earlier, I was assured by the recruiter that the annual bonus would make up for the cost of living gap. Even a

15% year wouldn't get me there.

Obviously you shouldn't anticipate the best possible year for a bonus, even if the recruiter says otherwise. Take the sage advice from mutual fund prospectuses: "past performance does not necessarily predict future results." Be sure to at least make note of what things look like with a 0% bonus. Ask the recruiters, managers, and any employees you talk to what the bonus percentages for the past few years were.

Most important of all: don't forget the taxes that will be taken out of any bonus. I'm happy to have a bonus plan, but I ultimately value these at zero as well.

Sign on Bonus

The sign on bonus is a one-time payment made to the employee, typically in their first paycheck. The sign on bonus might seem like a nice way the new employer can compensate you for the risk of a new job. It might, except that you usually have to repay the bonus if you leave the company before a certain time period. The bonuses I've seen require one year of service before you can quit or be fired without repaying the sum.

In summary, the sign on bonus is nice, but it usually won't help you if you get fired early on. I consider the sign on bonus to be compensation, but because it is paid only once, I amortize it over the two or three years I typically spend at a company.

For example, if I'm offered a $30,000 sign on bonus, I'll divide it by two years and treat an additional $15,000 as part of the annual compensation. If there are direct expenses related to this job, like relocation, I'll subtract those from the amount (plus additional for taxes) before figuring out the contribution to my salary.

Titles

Titles may not seem important, but they can have an impact on your career. This is a topic that is on the intangible side, so I'll save my thoughts for a future essay.

---

[1] http://online.wsj.com/articles/SB10000872396390443720204578004980476429190

[2] http://www.businessinsider.com/how-liquidation-preferences-work-2014-3

[3] http://www.investopedia.com/articles/stocks/07/ipo_lockup.asp

CHAPTER NINE

Happiness

There is one very good reason to take a job without an increase in pay: happiness. That's a subject big enough for another essay, and something that should be carefully evaluated separately from the economics.

Just like your job probably has the largest impact on your financial situation, it has one of the largest impacts on your overall happiness as well. You'll spend about a third of every year at work, so it makes sense to have a job that aligns with your interests and gives you a sense of accomplishment.

One of my worst jobs was a great fit for my skills. The company had a mission that could have had a large positive impact its potential customer base. Unfortunately, the folks in charge at the company were focused on the product instead of the mission. The product was a challenge, but it was developing fine. The biggest challenges, like funding and developing a market, were left up to fate. I hated the feeling of building something really great, but not believing that the company would be successful either financially or at achieving its mission. The situation made me miserable.

The situation of a job can make you more or less happy too. A bad boss can make your life miserable. Nothing has motivated me to leave a job faster than a boss that I didn't like. Even the work environment can harm you. This article mentions that job strain had a similar impact on health as smoking[1]! How much of a raise would you need to persuade you to take up smoking?

Your job can have an indirect impact on your happiness as well. This study shows how a daily commute impacts happiness[2]. Take particular note that the study found that higher pay didn't make up for a poor commute.

I don't think there is anything wrong with accepting a job offer that compensates you less if it will make you happier. Likewise, it makes sense to pass up an increase in compensation to stay at work that will make you happier.

---

[1] http://news.bbc.co.uk/2/hi/health/763401.stm

[2] http://www.theguardian.com/news/datablog/2014/feb/12/how-does-commuting-affect-wellbeing

CHAPTER TEN

Conclusions

Before you're ready to accept a new job offer, you've hopefully considered your job offer from many different angles. You've explored the possible risks of the new job, and compared the costs of living at the new job, the value of the benefits, and the value of any equity in the bargain.

You have all the data. Now you just need to make a decision. Lucky for you, a job offer is not a yes/no decision.

There is a third option in every negotiation: "You'll have to do better than that." It's a line I learned from Secrets of Power Negotiating by Roger Dawson. It really works.

One recruiter sent me a LinkedIn message out the blue. It was for a position in San Francisco with a "competitive salary." I asked him what the salary range was. He replied that the top of the range was $165,000. I messaged back "Sorry, you'd have to do better than that" and was immediately told they could do $185,000. That's a 12% increase and I hadn't even discussed my experience, much less interviewed. Those magic words can pay.

If you look at the numbers and decide to ask them to do better, be prepared for their response. If their recruiter is a good negotiator, they may ask you to justify your numbers. The recruiter might also ask you what they have to offer you to get you to say yes. If you've already gone through the process I've outlined, it won't be difficult to explain why the offer isn't good enough.

You should also be prepared for the recruiter to decide not to do better. Many software developers undervalue themselves, or simply aren't aware of how to properly evaluate a job offer. As a consequence, many companies have learned that they can hire a developer at the price they want by just making enough offers to different candidates. I've personally experienced this, and it's not fun saying "no" to a job that looks like a lot of fun, but which offered significantly lower compensation than the job I had. It's even more difficult when you've flown out for an interview, met the team, joked around with them, and had a great time. It was difficult, but I did say no.

Hopefully your decision won't be that difficult. Hopefully you have an offer that you can give an enthusiastic "yes" to, and your new job will make you happy and open new doors for you. Just make sure to consider compensation, benefits, equity, and intangibles like happiness when making that big decision.

Now you know as much as I do about job offers for software developers. If you'd like an easy way to use what you've just read, you can use my calculation spreadsheet to examine and compare job offers. Simply fill out your email at http://eepurl.com/9c5z5 and I'll send you the spreadsheet.